FROM SEA to SHINING SEA

FLORIDA

BARBARA A. SOMERVILL

Consultants

MELISSA N. MATUSEVICH, PH.D.
Curriculum and Instruction Specialist
Blacksburg, Virginia

JANA R. FINE
Youth Services Manager
Clearwater Public Library System
Clearwater, Florida

CHILDREN'S PRESS®
AN IMPRINT OF SCHOLASTIC INC.

New York • Toronto • London • Auckland • Sydney • Mexico City
New Delhi • Hong Kong • Danbury, Connecticut

Florida is the southernmost of the states in the region called the South. Other states in this region include Alabama, Arkansas, Delaware, Georgia, Kentucky, Louisiana, Maryland, Mississippi, North Carolina, South Carolina, Tennessee, Virginia, and West Virginia.

Project Editor: Lewis K. Parker
Art Director: Marie O'Neill
Photo Researcher: Marybeth Kavanagh
Design: Robin West, Ox and Company, Inc.
Page 6 map and recipe art: Susan Hunt Yule
All other maps: XNR Productions, Inc.

Library of Congress Cataloging in-Publication Data

Somervill, Barbara A.
    Florida/by Barbara A. Somervill.
       p. cm.—(From sea to shining sea)
    Includes bibliographical references and index.
       ISBN 0-531-18802-7
1. Florida—Juvenile literature. I. Title. II. Series

F311.3.S67 2008
975.9—dc22   2007037301

TABLE of CONTENTS

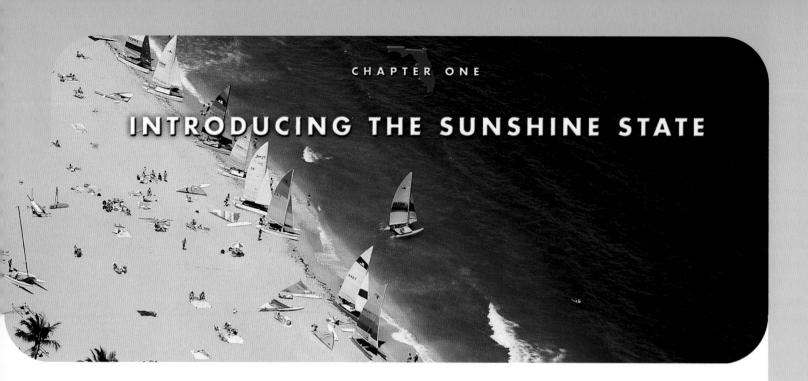

CHAPTER ONE

INTRODUCING THE SUNSHINE STATE

This scene from Fort Lauderdale shows that many people enjoy the surf, sun, and sailboats found in Florida.

When you think of Florida, two things probably come to mind—beaches and Walt Disney World. That's not surprising, because those are often the two major reasons that people vacation in Florida. The state's nickname—the Sunshine State—comes from the fact that Florida is warm and sunny, even in the winter. However, there is more to the Sunshine State than white sands and vacations. Florida is home to more than 15 million people. Only California, New York, and Texas have more people.

Florida is farther south than any other state except Hawaii. Draw a line around a globe at twenty-five degrees north latitude. Your line will pass through Saudi Arabia; the Sahara Desert; Egypt; Baja, Mexico—and the Florida Keys. Unlike many other places along your line, Florida is wet, warm, and alive with plants and animals.

Florida's state seal shows the state's history, culture, and beauty. Blue skies and rays of sunshine fill the background. On the left, a Seminole woman scatters flowers over the water. The tree shown is the state tree, the sabal palm. The steamboat represents Florida's economy or business.

What can you find in Florida?

- Both crocodiles and alligators living together
- At least twenty major league baseball teams holding spring training
- More than 3,500 kinds of wild plants, including lots of palm trees and cactus and delicate orchids
- Roller coasters called Gwazi, Montu, and Kumba at Busch Gardens
- A fast-action water ski show at Cypress Gardens
- Mickey Mouse and other fun characters at Walt Disney World
- Scuba diving and sailboating in warm, tropical waters
- Stock car and motorcycle racing at Daytona International Speedway

The Sunshine State has a rich and colorful history. It is more than just 1,350 miles (2,172 kilometers) of sandy beaches. It is more than just theme parks. In this book, you'll read about the people, places, and events that make Florida truly the Sunshine State.

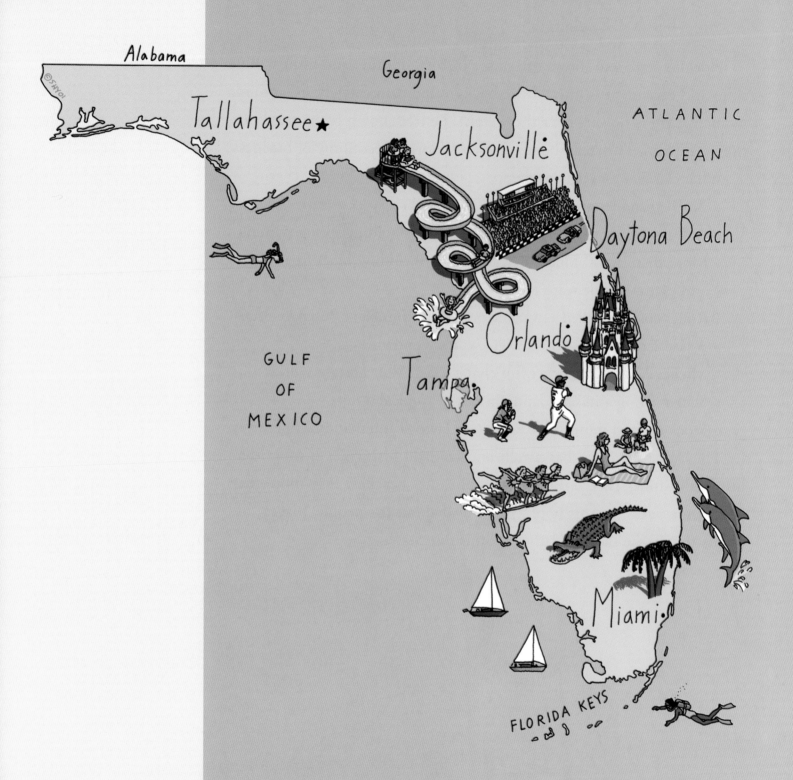

Alabama

Georgia

ATLANTIC OCEAN

Tallahassee ★

Jacksonville

Daytona Beach

GULF OF MEXICO

Orlando

Tampa

Miami

FLORIDA KEYS

CHAPTER TWO

THE LAND OF FLORIDA

Florida is the farthest south of mainland United States. To the north and northwest are Georgia and Alabama. The Atlantic Ocean provides Florida's eastern border. To the west is the Gulf of Mexico.

All this water keeps Florida warm and wet. Yet, water is one of the state's biggest problems. In all, Florida has 11,821 square miles (30,616 sq km) of water. However, not all of this water is drinkable. Florida's fresh water is being used up by the state's growing population.

Florida is flat. Its highest point is only 345 feet (105 meters) above sea level, and many places are barely ten feet (3 m) above sea level. Many skyscrapers in Miami are higher than the highest natural point in the state. However, billions of years ago, Florida was actually a string of underwater mountains. Seawater slowly wore away the mountains, leaving the flat land Florida is today.

The glow of the sunset adds even more warmth to Key Largo in the Florida Keys.

The total area of Florida is 65,755 square miles (170,304 sq km). The state ranks twenty-third in size. Florida is long—more than 500 miles (805 km) from the Georgia border to Florida's southern tip. The state is also narrow. It is just 361 miles (581 km) at its widest spot. There is no place in the state that is more than 60 miles (97 km) from a beach. Florida is a peninsula, a piece of land bounded on three sides by water. Along the top, where the state joins the mainland United States, is a stretch of land called the panhandle.

The state has five land regions: the coastal lowlands, the Everglades, the central highlands, the northwestern highlands, and the Marianna lowlands. Each region has its own special features.

Much of the northern panhandle is wilderness that has not been spoiled by humans.

Central and Northwestern Highlands

The central and northwestern highlands cover the panhandle and the center of the state. The uplands feature fresh-water springs, lakes, and sinkholes. A sinkhole forms when water dissolves limestone under the topsoil. When the topsoil drops, a hole is created. The largest sinkhole in the state is 320 feet (97 m) wide and 150 feet (46 m) deep. You could drop six cars and a house into a sinkhole that deep! At Falling Waters, near Chipley, a waterfall plunges into a 100-foot (31 m) sinkhole. Among the larger lakes in the central and northern highlands are Apopka, Ocklawaha, Talquin, and Harris. Rivers in this area include the Suwannee River, the Withlacoochee River, and the Apalachicola River.

Coastal Regions

Florida's 1,350 statute miles (2,173 km) of coastline stretches from the border with Georgia in the northeast, around the peninsula, and over to Alabama in the northwest. Along the shore are sandbars, coral reefs, and long, narrow islands, or keys, where fish, crabs, and shrimp live.

FIND OUT MORE

Some of Florida's most interesting animals first developed millions of years ago: alligators, manatees, loggerhead turtles, horse-shoe crabs, and seahorses. Why do you think these kinds of creatures have survived so long in Florida?

Sea oats sprout on the sandy beach of Sanibel Island.

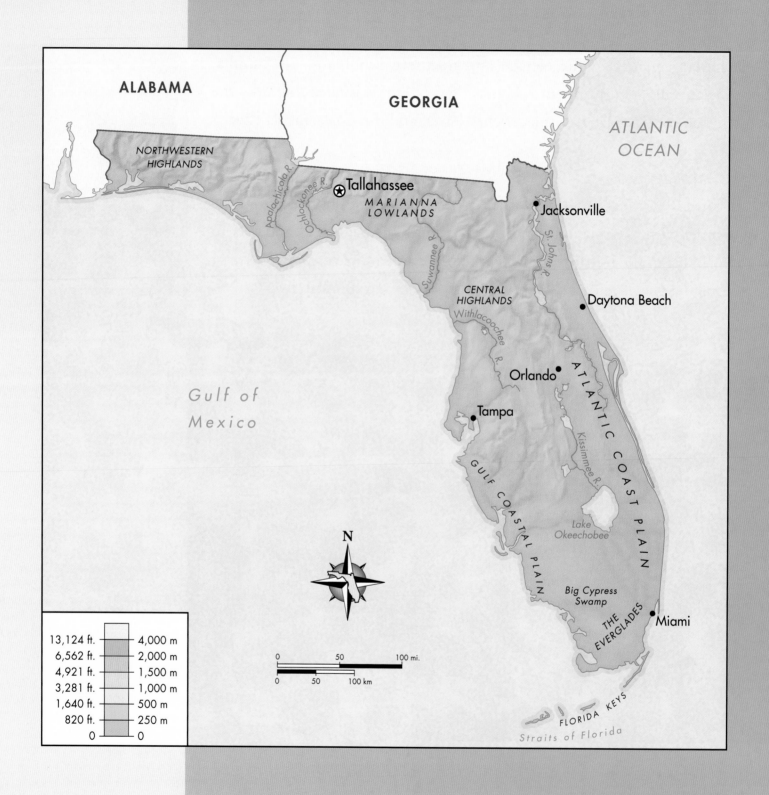

ALABAMA

GEORGIA

ATLANTIC
OCEAN

NORTHWESTERN
HIGHLANDS

Apalachicola R.

Ochlockonee R.

⊛ Tallahassee

MARIANNA
LOWLANDS

Suwannee R.

Jacksonville

St. Johns R.

CENTRAL
HIGHLANDS

Daytona Beach

Withlacoochee R.

Orlando

ATLANTIC COAST PLAIN

Tampa

Gulf of
Mexico

Kissimmee R.

GULF COASTAL PLAIN

Lake
Okeechobee

N

Big Cypress
Swamp

THE
EVERGLADES

Miami

FLORIDA KEYS

Straits of Florida

13,124 ft.	4,000 m
6,562 ft.	2,000 m
4,921 ft.	1,500 m
3,281 ft.	1,000 m
1,640 ft.	500 m
820 ft.	250 m
0	0

0   50   100 mi.

0   50   100 km

The Florida Keys stretch out from the state mainland toward the Caribbean country of Cuba.

The Florida Keys is a chain of 3,000 small islands that stretch out about 150 miles (241 km) into the ocean. These islands are coral reefs that cover limestone rock. The last of the islands is about 90 miles (145 km) from the island nation of Cuba.

The Everglades

Big Cypress Swamp, Lake Okeechobee, and the Everglades cover most of the southern part of Florida. Lake Okeechobee is both the state's largest and shallowest lake. Its average depth is only six to ten feet (2–3 m). However, the lake's water covers an area of about 700 square miles (1,813 sq km).

FIND OUT MORE

The word *key* comes from the Spanish word *cayo*, meaning "small island." Why might so many places in Florida have Spanish names?

Many tourists enjoy taking a guided tour of the Everglades.

The water from Lake Okeechobee empties into the Everglades—the largest swamp in the world. It is a sea of water grasses, cypress forests, and mangrove swamps. The Everglades is actually a very wide and shallow river. It is about 40 miles (64 km) wide, but you could wade through the swamp because it is only about six inches (15 centimeters) deep.

The Everglades and Big Cypress Swamp are home to hundreds of types of plants, animals, and birds. Cougars, black bears, raccoons, and deer live in the swamp. The wetter areas are marshes, where alligators, turtles, manatees, and crocodiles live. Many birds nest here, including herons, ibises, kites, turkey vultures, roseate spoonbills, and brown pelicans.

FIND OUT MORE

In 1947 the Everglades became a national park. Animals and birds cannot be hunted in the park. Plants and trees cannot be cleared away to build homes. Why do you think the Everglades is protected in this way?

An American alligator strolls through a swamp in southern Florida.

Marianna Lowlands

The Marianna lowlands lie in the north-central section of Florida's panhandle. These lowlands have soft, rolling hills where there are many sinkholes and caverns.

CLIMATE

Florida has hot, humid summers and mild winters. The average July temperatures in Miami run from 76°F (24°C) at night to 89°F (32°C) during the day. Orlando's average July temperatures range from a pleasant 71°F (22°C) to a sizzling 91°F (33°C). January temperatures across the state average 60°F (16°C).

EXTRA! EXTRA!

The Everglades kite bird only eats apple snails. When the Everglades become dry during periods of little rain, apple snails die out and the population of kite birds decreases.

Hurricanes strike Florida almost every year. These powerful storms usually start in the Atlantic Ocean near Africa. By the time a hurricane hits Florida, its winds can reach over 100 miles per hour (160 kph). Often, people must leave their homes and move to safety far from a hurricane's path.

The National Hurricane Center in Miami keeps Florida—and the rest of the nation—alert to hurricane danger. In 1992, Hurricane Andrew struck southern Florida. Early warning by the National Hurricane Center saved many lives. However, property damage was as high as $20 billion and thirty-eight people were killed by this terrible hurricane.

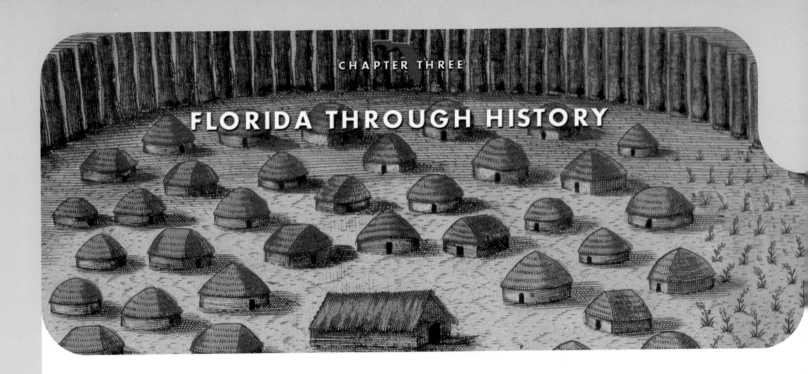

CHAPTER THREE

FLORIDA THROUGH HISTORY

People first arrived in Florida about 10,000 years ago. Today, we call these people hunter-gatherers because of how they found their food. They *hunted* animals and *gathered* berries, fruits, and nuts. When food became scarce in one area, the people moved on. They didn't build villages; instead, they camped near their food supply.

By 3000 B.C., hunter-gatherer clans started building villages along the coast. The main food for these people was shellfish. When they finished eating, they tossed the leftover shells into piles near their homes. Scientists study the shell mounds to learn about these early Floridians.

By 1500, more than 10,000 Native Americans lived in what is now called Florida. These people formed five main tribes. The Calusa settled along the Atlantic Coast. The Tequesta lived in the south. The Ais settled in central Florida along the Atlantic. The Timucua lived in the

This drawing shows a circular Timucuan village. These Native Americans built cone-shaped houses made of palm branches and vines.

central and northeastern parts of what is now Florida. The Apalachee were farmers and hunters in the northwest (Pensacola area). Two smaller tribes—the Arawaks and the Matecumbes—lived in the Florida Keys.

SPANISH EXPLORERS ARRIVE

In 1498, Henry Cabot traveled around present-day Florida, and produced the first rough map of the peninsula's outline. No one knows if Cabot actually landed in today's Florida, although it would be reasonable to think he did land for food and water.

However, history tells us the first European to land is Juan Ponce de León, in 1513. Many people think Ponce de León was searching for the Fountain of Youth when he landed in Florida. This is not true. Like most Spanish explorers, Ponce de León was looking for gold. He was disappointed. There were no golden cities in Florida.

Ponce de León named the area *La Florida*, Spanish for "full of flowers." When he arrived, it was Easter week, called *Pascua Florida* in Spanish. No attempt was made to set up a village at that time. Eight years later, Ponce de León returned to Florida to start a colony. Native Americans fought against Ponce de León, who was hurt

WHO'S WHO IN FLORIDA?

Juan Ponce de León (1460–1521) was a Spanish explorer. In 1493, he sailed with Christopher Columbus on Columbus's second voyage. In 1513, he explored the east coast of present-day Florida, then returned to Spain.

in the battle and soon died from his wounds. Some of Ponce de León's men escaped to Puerto Rico to the south.

More Spaniards came to Florida in the 1500s. Both Pánfilo de Narvaéz and Hernando de Soto explored the west coast of Florida, near present-day Tampa. However, starting a settlement was difficult. Heat, mosquitoes, and disease were not easy to deal with. Also, local native tribes resisted the Spaniards who wanted to take their land.

In 1559, Tristan de Luna set off from Mexico with a group of about 1,500 people. They planned to set up a town near present-day Pensacola. Unfortunately, a hurricane destroyed the colony in 1560. Those who survived the hurricane soon returned to Mexico.

De Soto landed in Florida, then marched northwest to become the first European to discover the Mississippi River.

THE FRENCH BUILD A FORT

In 1562, Jean Ribault led the first French exploration of Florida. Landing on the eastern coast, Ribault placed a marble marker, or stone, near the mouth of the Saint Johns River to show the French claim to the area. Two years later, a group of French Huguenots established the Fort Caroline colony near where Jacksonville is located today.

The Huguenots were Protestants who lived in France from about 1500–1700. In the late 1500s, many Huguenots were murdered by the French government under Queen Catherine. Huguenots fled France and went to England, Holland, and North America looking for freedom. They settled in Florida, South Carolina, New York, and Virginia.

THE SPANISH CLAIM FLORIDA

From Columbus's first voyage in 1492, the Spanish claimed large areas of North America. Spanish kings grew rich from gold and gems that Spanish explorers brought back from Mexico. Philip II of Spain was angry when he heard about the French settlement. Not wanting to share the riches of North America with France, he sent 400 soldiers to force the French to leave. Led by Pedro Menéndez de Avilés, the troops attacked Fort Caroline and killed the French set-

FAMOUS FIRSTS

- First permanent European settlement, Saint Augustine, 1565
- First newspaper printed in Florida, the *East Florida Gazette*, Saint Augustine, 1783
- First naval battle of the Civil War, Pensacola, 1861
- First alligator farm, Anastasia Island, 1892
- First national bird preserve, Pelican Island, 1903
- First porpoise born in captivity, Marineland, 1940
- First American astronaut to orbit Earth, Floridian John Glenn, 1962

tlers. On September 8, 1565, Menéndez de Avilés settled the first permanent European city in North America, Saint Augustine.

The arrival of Europeans was the beginning of the end for Florida's Native Americans. The tribes fought to keep their land, but could not defeat the Spanish. Many native people died in these battles. Others were captured by Europeans and sold as slaves. Still others died from diseases such as small pox and measles. Within 250 years, the tribes were wiped out. Because they left no written information, only shell mounds and accounts written by their European conquerors tell us about their lives.

The remains of oyster-shell heaps are the only evidence of Native Americans who once lived on Fort George Island.

THE ENGLISH WANT FLORIDA

The English settled the Carolinas in 1663. Once again, Spain faced a new threat in Florida. Within five years, Englishman Robert Searles raided the city of Saint Augustine, killed more than 100 people, and sold all Native Americans there into slavery.

The English wanted more and more land. The Carolinas grew larger as the British took land that belonged to Spain. The Spanish protested. England and Spain solved the problem through the Treaty of Madrid in 1670, which set a border between Florida and the Carolinas just north of the Savannah River. Today, the Savannah River serves as the border between South Carolina and Georgia.

England gained possession of Florida in 1763 from the Spanish. During the 1700s, control of Florida changed often between the Spanish and the English. By the end of the American Revolutionary War (1775–1783), Florida was controlled by Spain. Between 1783 and 1819, Spain kept its hold on Florida, although English settlers continued to live in the region.

THE WAR OF 1812

In 1812, war broke out between Britain and the United States. Britain had been stopping U.S. ships on the seas, taking sailors off the ships, and forcing them to work on British ships. Even though Florida was a Spanish colony, the British took over Pensacola and made it a naval base. General Andrew Jackson led his troops against British forces in November 1814. Pensacola was burned, but the city was freed from British control.

THE SEMINOLE WAR

As more Americans began to move into Florida, they encountered Native Americans who called themselves Seminoles. The Seminole tribe was not a true tribe such as the Timucua or the Apalachee. Instead, it was a mix of native and African people fleeing slavery in the southern United States. The tribe was made up of Creek, Yemasee, and runaway slaves. The group was called *sim-in-o-li*, which means "wild people."

The Americans and the Seminoles disagreed over runaway slaves. Following laws in the United States, the U.S. Army wanted to return Seminoles of African descent to slavery. The tribe refused to allow the army to take their African members away. This disagreement led to the First Seminole War

This drawing captures the struggle of the Seminoles as Osceola led them in an attack on Fort King in 1835.

WHO'S WHO IN FLORIDA?

Osceola (1804?–1838) was born a Red Stick Creek. He came to live among the Seminoles as a child. Osceola led the Seminoles in an attack against the U.S. Army. The U.S. Army arrested Osceola even though he held a white flag of truce, and took him prisoner. He died in prison in South Carolina.

(1817–1818). Although Florida was controlled by Spain, Andrew Jackson led American soldiers into Florida to fight the Seminoles. As a result of this war, the Creeks gave a large part of their land in Florida to the Americans.

FLORIDA BECOMES A TERRITORY

Under the Adams-Onís Treaty, on February 22, 1819, Spain gave Florida to the United States once and for all. Before this time, there were two sections of Florida. Saint Augustine was the capital of East Florida, and Pensacola was the capital of West Florida. The new territory, called Florida Territory, put its capital halfway between the two cities—in Tallahassee. On March 4, 1824, Tallahassee became the official territorial capital. Andrew Jackson became the first territorial governor.

A Second Seminole War (1835–1842) started when the U.S. government tried to move the Seminoles to Indian Territory in what is now Oklahoma. Chief Osceola led the Seminoles in a fight against moving west. The Seminoles raided settlements and forts. American soldiers burned Seminole villages and killed men, women, and children. Although most Seminoles were captured, taken from their homes, and sent west, some moved deeper into the center of Florida. The largest battle of the war took place on December 25, 1837. About one thousand American soldiers fought and defeated about five hundred Seminoles. When the war ended, less than a hundred Seminoles were left in the Everglades.

STATEHOOD

By 1845, slavery in the United States was an important issue. Slaves, originally brought from Africa, were forced against their will to do work that their white owners did not want to do. As unpaid workers, they were treated as property by their owners and had no freedoms or rights. Slaves were severely punished for disobeying their owners. The Northern states had abolished, or done away with, slavery, but slavery and the slave trade still continued in the Southern states. At the time, slaves were considered essential to the South's economy.

An important problem faced by the U.S. Congress was how to admit new states to the Union to keep a balance between free and slave states. The South wanted to have an equal number of slave and free states so that the North would not have too much power. Florida entered the United States as a slave state on March 3, 1845. At that time, there were fifteen free states and twelve slave states. Tallahassee remained the capital city. William Moseley became the first governor of the state of Florida.

In Florida, white plantation owners thought they could not survive without slaves to work their farms. In 1845 Florida lawmakers made freeing slaves illegal, unless individual owners helped their ex-slaves leave the state. An 1858 law allowed free African-Americans to choose masters and become slaves again. Not surprisingly, few free African-Americans thought this was a good idea.

Abraham Lincoln, a politician in Illinois, had spoken out against allowing slavery to spread to new U.S. territories. When Lincoln was elected president in 1860, many people in the southern states began to worry. They were afraid that Lincoln would take away their state rights to slave ownership and bring about an end to slavery. The South depended on cotton and tobacco grown on large farms or plantations for their economy. Many Southerners thought that only slave labor made growing crops profitable. The economy in the north was based on manufacturing products. People worked in factories and were paid wages. The South also felt that state governments should be stronger than the federal government, while the North believed in a stronger federal government. These differences led to a Civil War (1861–1865).

On January 10, 1861, Florida seceded from the United States. Florida, along with several other southern states, joined a new country called the Confederate States of

EXTRA! EXTRA!

In May 1864, a small group of elderly men and young boys defended Tallahassee from the Union Army at the Battle of Natural Bridge. Although outnumbered and outgunned, the Floridians turned back the Union soldiers. Austin, Texas, and Tallahassee were the only Confederate state capitals that the Union Army never captured.

This scene along the Saint Johns River shows the gunboat *Columbine* being captured in 1864.

America on February 4, 1861. The country was at war. Early in the Civil War, Union troops captured most of the cities along the coast.

At least 15,000 Florida men fought on the Confederate side during the war. In all, 5,000 people died, and at least 5,000 more were wounded in battle. Florida also contributed food, such as beef, sugar, and fish, to the Confederate cause. The Confederate Army finally surrendered its troops in 1865.

After the war, the U.S. government set particular terms that each Confederate state had to meet before being allowed to join the Union again. In the beginning, Florida refused to agree to the Union terms. In 1868, Florida finally accepted

FIND OUT MORE

The Fourteenth Amendment to the U.S. Constitution says all persons born in the United States and subject to its laws are U.S. citizens. These citizens have equal protection under the law. Why might many Floridians have opposed the Fourteenth Amendment?

the Fourteenth Amendment to the Constitution of the United States. This amendment, or change, gave citizenship rights to former slaves. On June 25, 1868, Florida again became part of the United States. However, the state government, controlled by white men, passed laws that kept African-Americans from enjoying the rights of most Americans. Their right to vote, own property, and even move about freely were extremely limited.

THE SPANISH-AMERICAN WAR

As the 1800s came to a close, the United States once again faced war—this time with Spain. The war had several causes. At that time, Cuba was a colony of Spain. Cuba, a small island just south of Florida, was struggling against Spain for independence, much as the United States fought Britain in the Revolutionary War. Many people in the United States wanted Cuba to be free. In addition, Spain supposedly sank a U.S. battleship, called the *Maine,* in the harbor of Havana, Cuba. Articles about the sinking of the ship appeared in newspapers and Americans were angry that Spain had dared to attack a U.S. ship. In April 1898, the U.S. declared war on Spain. The Spanish-American War (1898) began.

Cuba is only about 100 miles (160 km) from the southern tip of Florida. Many troops were shipped from Florida ports to Cuba for the fighting. Miami and Tampa became camps for training troops. The war lasted only a few weeks. The Treaty of Paris, which ended the war, gave the United States Puerto Rico, the Philippines, and Guam. Cuba was free from Spanish rule. Once the war had ended, many soldiers and sailors brought their families to Florida to live.

TWENTIETH-CENTURY FLORIDA

As the 1900s began, Florida enjoyed progress and change. Large mineral deposits were discovered, mined, and sold. Railroads criss-crossed the state, opening southern Florida to people moving south. Refrigerated trains allowed oranges and grapefruits to be shipped across the United States. As these crops became more popular throughout the nation, they became more important to the state's economy.

Several business owners, including Henry M. Flagler and Henry B. Plant, built railroads and hotels in Florida. Flagler built a railroad connecting points on the Florida east coast from Jacksonville to Miami. He also built a chain of luxurious hotels to attract travelers to Florida. Flagler just about created the city of Miami when he built roads, an electric plant, and water and sewer lines. He changed Miami from a little town of a few stone buildings and shacks into a place where visitors would want to go.

Plant built a railroad, the Plant Railroad System, from northern Florida down the peninsula. Now Florida was open on the Gulf Coast from Jacksonville to Tampa.

WHO'S WHO IN FLORIDA?

Henry Flagler (1830–1913) built the Florida East Coast Railway between Jacksonville and the Florida Keys. Flagler also built hotels in Saint Augustine, Miami, and Palm Beach.

Flagler's railroad was built on a long bridge across the Florida Keys. He opened up the islands to tourists.

Plant also built large hotels. By spending money to improve state transportation and industry, these men helped Florida grow. Besides better transportation, there was an invention that helped build southern Florida—the air conditioner. Air conditioning made southern Florida's hot, sweaty summers bearable.

World War I (1914–1918) brought opportunity to Florida in two ways. Naval bases in Pensacola and Mayport (near Jacksonville) became training sites and ports for war ships. Florida also provided oranges, grapefruits, and other vegetables for feeding our soldiers overseas.

During the early 1920s, Florida's economy grew tremendously. Land prices rose, and cities exploded with new residents. For example, only 1,681 people lived in Miami in 1900. By 1925, that number had jumped to 69,754. Overall, Florida's population grew from 140,424 in 1860 to 4,951,580 in 1960—a growth rate of more than 3,500 percent in 100 years.

In the 1920s, advertisements appeared in Northern cities that portrayed Florida as a paradise where people could relax under palm trees on golden beaches. Many Northerners began buying property in Florida on which to retire or to vacation. Real estate companies and landowners were getting rich. People from all over the country were buying up land just to sell it to other people who wanted to purchase land. They wanted to get rich, too. Some people were using every cent in their bank accounts or borrowing money to buy land in Florida. Lots of people believed the advertisements and were buying land that they hadn't even seen or land that hadn't even been developed—stretches of swampland or acres of scrubby pine trees.

After a few years, land developers, realizing the high costs of draining swamps and building cities, began to back out of deals. The sales of land suddenly ended. Money stopped rolling into Florida. Land prices crashed to record lows in 1926. In January 1926, a ship that was used as a floating hotel became stuck in Miami's ship channel. It blocked shipping for a month. People couldn't sell their goods and people couldn't get to Miami by ship. However, since the prices of railroad tickets had also increased, the cheapest way to get to Miami was by ship. Because many people couldn't pay for their land now, banks began to take over the loans and the land. Suddenly there were dozens of unsold lots in Miami.

Then, in September, a hurricane struck. Winds of 132 miles per hour snapped telephone poles and lifted up a huge ship and set it down in the center of Miami. The hurricane killed hundreds of people and left 47,000 people homeless. Newcomers to Florida had never encountered anything like a hurricane. For the next few weeks, roads were packed with people heading north. After ten years of booming economy, Florida went bust.

When a powerful hurricane struck the Miami area in 1926, it destroyed homes and businesses.

30

Three years later, in 1929, the Great Depression started. Along with the rest of the country, Florida businesses closed and thousands of workers lost their jobs. Families lost their homes, and many people were left with nothing.

The arrival of World War II (1939–1945) brought the country out of the Great Depression. Pensacola, once only a naval base, became a naval air station. More than two million military people trained in the state. At one point, a German submarine secretly landed German spies on the beaches near Jacksonville. These spies were quickly arrested when they arrived in the town.

After the war, Florida once again enjoyed a booming economy. Cities grew as transportation improved. A new interstate highway system was built so that it was possible to drive from the northern areas of the state to Miami. Tourism also exploded, as Northerners headed for Florida beaches in the winter.

Another new industry began in Florida—aerospace. In 1950, the United States began sending up rockets from Cape Canaveral. In the early 1960s, satellites were put into orbit above Earth, and soon manned space flights took place. In 1969, Neil Armstrong and Edwin Aldrin became the first men to walk on the moon. Not all space efforts were suc-

WHAT'S IN A NAME?

Many names of places in Florida have interesting origins.

Name	Comes From or Means
Florida	Spanish for "feast of flowers"
Tallahassee	Native American for "old fields" or "old town"
Key West	Spanish, *cayo hueso* which means "island of bones"
Jacksonville	For Andrew Jackson, first Florida Territory governor
Osceola county	For Osceola, leader of the Seminoles
Frostproof	Because the temperature there never reaches below freezing
Boca Raton	Spanish for "mouse's mouth," based on the shape of the coastline

WHO'S WHO IN FLORIDA?

Lue Gim Gong (1858–1955), a Chinese-American scientist, developed a kind of orange that resisted frost. This orange also ripened later in the season so that growers could ship their fruit to northern markets throughout the year.

cessful, however. In 1986, the space shuttle *Challenger* burst into flames on take-off, killing all the astronauts aboard.

Starting in the late 1950s and on into the 1980s, Florida faced a new problem—thousands of Cubans coming into the state. In 1959, a Communist government took over in Cuba. Many Cubans, who didn't want to live under a Communist system, came to the United States. In the 1970s and 1980s, many more people risked their lives to cross from Cuba to the United States in small boats and rafts. The largest of these groups was the Mariel boatlift in 1980. At the same time, people fled political unrest in Haiti, looking for a new life in Florida.

In 1980 Fidel Castro, the president of Cuba, opened up the port of Mariel so that Cubans could travel to the United States. Within a few months, more than 125,000 Cubans had fled to the United States.

Some Floridians welcomed the Cuban newcomers. Others felt that such large numbers of people strained resources in the state. They pointed out that these people needed places to live and proper medical care. The state government had to provide these services, with money from taxes that Florida's residents paid. Many newcomers had to be taught English. Although several large cities provided signs and other information in both English and Spanish, an amendment to the state constitution established English as Florida's official language in 1988.

Miami is a large city made up of several neighborhoods. Many Cubans first settled on Eighth Street and changed its name to "Calle Ocho," the Spanish term for Eighth Street. The area is now known as Little Havana. Other neighborhoods include Little Haiti and Little Managua.

The 1990s were marked by two natural disasters. In 1992, Hurricane Andrew raked across Florida. This hurricane killed 38 people and caused more than $20 billion in property damages. Hurricane Andrew also left 250,000 people without homes. Then, in 1998, more than 2,000 wildfires burned out of control from May through July. These fires destroyed at least 200,000 acres along the northeastern coastline. Experts estimated that the fires caused at least $278 million in property damage. About one hundred people—mostly firefighters—were injured in the fires.

In 1999 two events occurred that will continue to influence the lives of future Floridians. One, the state government and the federal government planned to work together to restore the Everglades. Parts of the Everglades had been drained so that houses and farms could be built. Pesticides and other pollution from farms and sugarcane fields also flowed into the swamp. Under the proposal, $7.8 billion would be used to make sure that the Everglades remained in a natural condition. That same year, Governor Jeb Bush signed a law to set up an education voucher program. Under this law, students from Florida's worst public schools could receive money from the state government to attend other schools, such as private or religious schools. People were not sure what effect vouchers would have on the public school system.

The national spotlight beamed on Florida, as well. On Thanksgiving Day, 1999, a six-year-old Cuban boy was rescued off the Florida coast. He, his mother, and ten other people had fled from Cuba on a small boat. The boy's mother and everyone else on the boat were killed when the boat sank. The boy, Elian Gonzalez, was temporarily turned over to his relatives in Miami. However, the U.S. government said that Elian had to be returned to Cuba to live with his father. Some people formed groups to protest the decision. They said that the boy should remain with his relatives in freedom in the United States. Other people said that Elian's father should be allowed to take him back to Cuba. Elian became famous as articles about him appeared almost every day in newspapers around the world. Finally, in April 2000, the U.S. Supreme Court refused

Elian Gonzalez plays outside his Miami relatives' home.

to hear an appeal by the boy's relatives and he left the United States with his father to return to Cuba. "Elian's mother brought him to this country with the hope and dreams of the Statue of Liberty," a spokesperson for Elian's family members in Miami said. "Now Elian Gonzalez cannot be free."

In 2000, Florida played an important role in electing George W. Bush as president of the United States. The outcome of the 2000 presidential election between Al Gore, the Democratic candidate, and George Bush, the Republican candidate, depended on who would

receive Florida's 25 electoral votes. Electoral votes are cast by a group of people who are chosen to represent the state of Florida in a Presidential election. Their votes reflect the votes of everyone in the state.

On election night, November 7, the first count of votes in Florida showed that Bush was ahead by 1,784 votes. Florida state law requires a recount of votes in such a close victory. Meanwhile, thousands of people claimed that the ballots were designed so badly that they voted for the wrong candidate and others said that they had tried to vote but were turned away from the polls. Arguments for and against accepting the vote recount or doing more recounts continued until the U.S. Supreme Court ruled on December 12 to stop any more counting of votes. On December 12, 2000, Al Gore gave up and Florida's electoral votes went to Bush, making him the president.

Going into the twenty-first century, Florida faces many difficult challenges. About 800 people a day move into Florida. This ever-growing population creates several problems for the state. It strains the state's freshwater resources to the maximum. Most freshwater is in the rural northern areas. However, water must be pumped to Florida's crowded cities, which are much farther south. In the future, Floridians will debate on the best ways to meet the water needs of people who live in the cities.

The growing population also causes problems with the natural environment. Thousands of people are moving into wilderness areas. For example, the Everglades is the largest subtropical wilderness in the United States. However, building cities and developing farmland near the Everglades drains and then floods the swamp to suit the needs of people and not the needs of the animals and plants that live there. Floridians need to work out plans to save the natural environment, yet still meet the needs of the growing population.

Many new residents are elderly people who have retired to Florida. Tens of thousands more retirees will come to Florida during this century. The state will need to figure out ways to meet the high cost of housing and medical care for these people.

Plans also need to be developed to move people to safe areas when powerful storms strike. The cost in destroyed property and the risk to human lives caused by hurricanes must be considered. New hurricanes each year damage more property and transportation routes. Even better

Deep in the heart of the Everglades, this roseate spoonbill feeds its chicks.

37

early-warning systems need to be developed to move residents to safer areas northward up the peninsula.

Florida must also consider the influx of immigrants to the state—at the rate of about three million every ten years. Thousands of people have already fled to Florida from Cuba and other nations in the Caribbean. In the future, more and more people will come to Florida in search of better lives. Florida must work out ways to meet the housing, education, and medical needs of these people and others who will follow them to the Sunshine State.

The strength of Florida is in the diversity of its population, and the future of Florida lies in its ability to handle its many resources. Environmental protection of water and land resources, improved economy, and social services for older Floridians must all be managed if Florida is to continue to thrive.

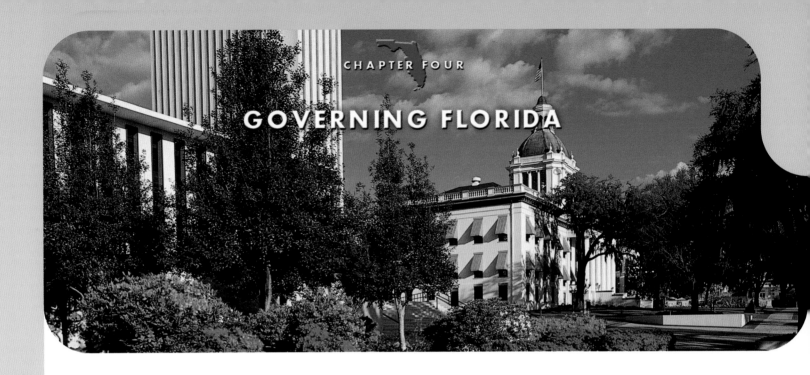

CHAPTER FOUR

GOVERNING FLORIDA

The plan for running the state government is set up in its constitution. Specific responsibilities or jobs are divided among three branches: the executive, the legislative, and the judicial. No one branch is more powerful than any other. This is called a "balance of power," and keeps the government running smoothly.

Florida's state capitol building—a 22-story skyscraper—towers over the Old Capitol. The New Capitol opened in 1977.

THE STATE CONSTITUTION

The current Florida constitution went into effect in 1969. Before that, the state had a territorial constitution (1839) and several state constitutions (1861, 1865, 1868, and 1869). To make a change—called an *amendment*—to the constitution, more than half of the voters must approve the change. Citizens can ask for a meeting to bring about changes in the state constitution. However, changes are usually suggested in the state legislature. These changes must pass both the Senate and the House of Representatives by three out of every five votes. Every change to the constitution is voted on by the legislature.

Governor Charlie Crist is dedicated to preserving Florida's famed Everglades ecosystem.

THE EXECUTIVE BRANCH

The governor is the chief executive of the state, much like the head coach of a team. The governor works with many people who are also part of the executive branch. Like a coach has assistant coaches, the governor of Florida has a group of people who offer advice on the economy, agriculture, the law, and education. This group of advisors is called the governor's cabinet.

Florida's governors appoint judges and members of the cabinet. The governor also commands the state national guard. If there is an emergency, such as a hurricane or a riot, the governor calls out the guard to protect the people.

Florida's governor makes sure that the state's laws are enforced. State governors serve four-year terms. In Florida, people vote separately for governor and lieutenant

FLORIDA GOVERNORS

Name	Term	Name	Term
William D. Moseley	1845–1849	Cary A. Hardee	1921–1925
Thomas Brown	1849–1853	John W. Martin	1925–1929
James E. Broome	1853–1857	Doyle E. Carlton	1929–1933
Madison S. Perry	1857–1861	David Sholtz	1933–1937
John Milton	1861–1865	Fred P. Cone	1937–1941
Abraham K. Allison	1865	Spessard L. Holland	1941–1945
William Marvin	1865–1866	Millard F. Caldwell	1945–1949
David S. Walker	1866–1868	Fuller Warren	1949–1953
Harrison Reed	1868–1873	Daniel T. McCarty	1953
Ossian B. Hart	1873–1874	Charley E. Johns	1953–1955
Marcellus L. Stearns	1874–1877	LeRoy Collins	1955–1961
George F. Drew	1877–1881	C. Farris Bryant	1961–1965
William D. Bloxham	1881–1885	W. Haydon Burns	1965–1967
Edward A. Perry	1885–1889	Claude R. Kirk, Jr.	1967–1971
Francis P. Fleming	1889–1893	Reubin O. Askew	1971–1979
Henry L. Mitchell	1893–1897	Robert D. Graham	1979–1987
William D. Bloxham	1897–1901	Wayne Mixson	1987
William S. Jennings	1901–1905	Bob Martinez	1987–1991
Napoleon B. Broward	1905–1909	Lawton M. Chiles, Jr.	1991–1998
Albert W. Gilchrist	1909–1913	Buddy MacKay	1998–1999
Park Trammell	1913–1917	John Ellis "Jeb" Bush	1999–2007
Sidney J. Catts	1917–1921	Charles Joseph "Charlie" Crist	2007–

governor, so it is possible for Floridians to have a Democratic governor and a Republican lieutenant governor, or the other way around.

THE LEGISLATIVE BRANCH

The legislature makes state laws. The legislature has two "houses" or groups: the Senate and the House of Representatives. The Senate has forty members who serve four-year terms. The House of Representatives has 120 members who serve two-year terms. State laws can cover almost any topic, such as taxes, education, real estate, ecology, or crimes. No state law, however, can take away rights that are promised in the Florida or U.S. Constitution.

THE JUDICIAL BRANCH

Judicial means "having to do with judges and courts." The judicial branch reviews laws to see whether they are fair and if they follow the rules of the state constitution. The laws are tested through trials in state courts.

The judicial system, or branch, is made up of different levels of courts. The highest, or most important, is the Florida Supreme Court. Governors choose judges to serve on the Florida Supreme Court. Justices (judges) serve for six-year terms. Other courts, called lower courts, include the state court of appeals, twenty circuit courts, and sixty-seven county courts. State attorneys general represent Florida's interests in criminal trials.

The easiest way to understand these courts is to follow a crime through the court system. A crime is committed. The criminal is caught and stands trial. If the crime is a minor crime, such as reckless driving, the trial is held in the county court. If the crime is a felony, or serious crime such as theft or murder, the trial is held in the state circuit court. A circuit court judge hears the trial, and a jury of twelve people decides if the defendant is guilty or not.

If the defendant is found guilty but thinks the trial was unfair, his or her lawyer files an appeal with the state court of appeals. An appeal asks the judicial system to review the trial. If the justices feel the trial was unfair, the defendant may go free. If the justices feel the trial was fair, the defendant has one more chance to have the case heard. This last hearing would be in the Florida Supreme Court where the justices decide if the law itself was fair or unfair.

TAKE A TOUR OF TALLAHASSEE, FLORIDA'S CAPITAL CITY

Although most of Florida's population lives in southern Florida, the state capital—Tallahassee—is in the north. It is only 14 miles (22.5 k) from the Georgia border. Tallahassee is a city of about 125,000 people. Most of these people are state or local government workers, such as lawyers, accountants, secretaries, and engineers.

Tallahassee's capitol building is a strange mix of the old and the new. Begun in 1826, the domed Old Capitol took several years to build.

FLORIDA STATE GOVERNMENT

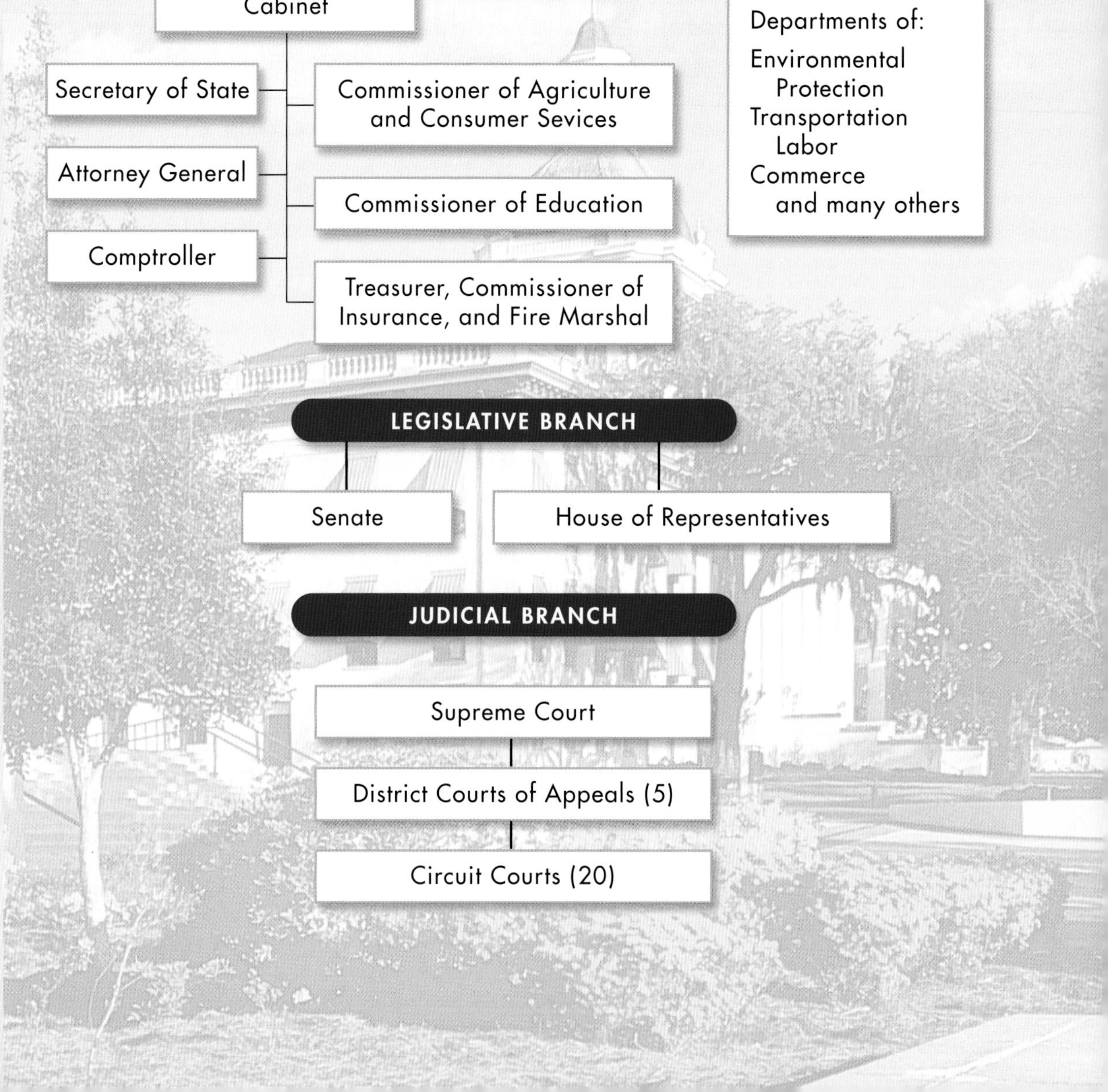

EXECUTIVE BRANCH

Governor

Lieutenant Governor

Cabinet

Departments of:

Environmental
Protection
Transportation
Labor
Commerce
and many others

Secretary of State

Commissioner of Agriculture and Consumer Sevices

Attorney General

Commissioner of Education

Comptroller

Treasurer, Commissioner of Insurance, and Fire Marshal

LEGISLATIVE BRANCH

Senate

House of Representatives

JUDICIAL BRANCH

Supreme Court

District Courts of Appeals (5)

Circuit Courts (20)

Today, the Old Capitol lies in the shadow of the New Capitol, built during the late 1970s. The New Capitol is a modern, twenty-two-story structure. From the New Capitol's observation deck on the twenty-second floor, visitors see as far away as the Gulf of Mexico and as close as the parks and gardens sprinkled throughout the city.

Not too far from the Old and New Capitols is the place where Hernando de Soto and his crew spent their first Christmas in North America in 1539. This was the site of the first Christmas celebration in North America. In 1986, scientists found copper coins at the De Soto Historic Site that are the oldest ever found in the United States.

This view of Tallahassee shows many of the city's tall buildings, including the capitol.

Tallahassee offers some other treats as well. You can stop by Bradley's Country Store for a sample of homemade sausage. You won't believe all the old T-birds, Cadillacs, and Corvettes at the Tallahassee Antique Car Museum. The museum even has two original Batmobiles from the movie "Batman Returns."

For art lovers, there is the Florida State University Museum of Fine Arts and the LeMoyne Center for Visual Arts. The paintings and sculptures at these sites will easily entertain visitors for an afternoon.

The Florida Museum of History brings alive the state's rich past from prehistoric times to the twentieth century. In this museum, you can see the skeleton of a mastodon, treasures from old Spanish ships, and a rebuilt steamboat. At the Tallahassee Museum of History and Natural Science, you can tour a farmhouse from the 1880s and see what life was like back then. You can also walk through the museum's Natural Habitat Zoo and see native Florida animals in their natural habitats, including panthers, red wolves, black bears, deer, and alligators.

Other sites well worth visiting are the Vietnam Veterans' Memorial near the state capitol, and Mission San Luis de Apalachee due west of the city. The monument at the Vietnam Veterans' Memorial has a 40-foot American flag flying between two granite towers. On the towers are the names of soldiers from Florida who died in the Vietnam War. Mission San Luis is the site of a Spanish and Indian village that was settled from 1656–1704.

For those who enjoy flowers and natural beauty, a walk through Tallahassee's Maclay Garden State Park is a must. There are more than

A mastodon skeleton stands inside the Museum of Florida History. It was recovered from Wakulla Springs in the 1930s.

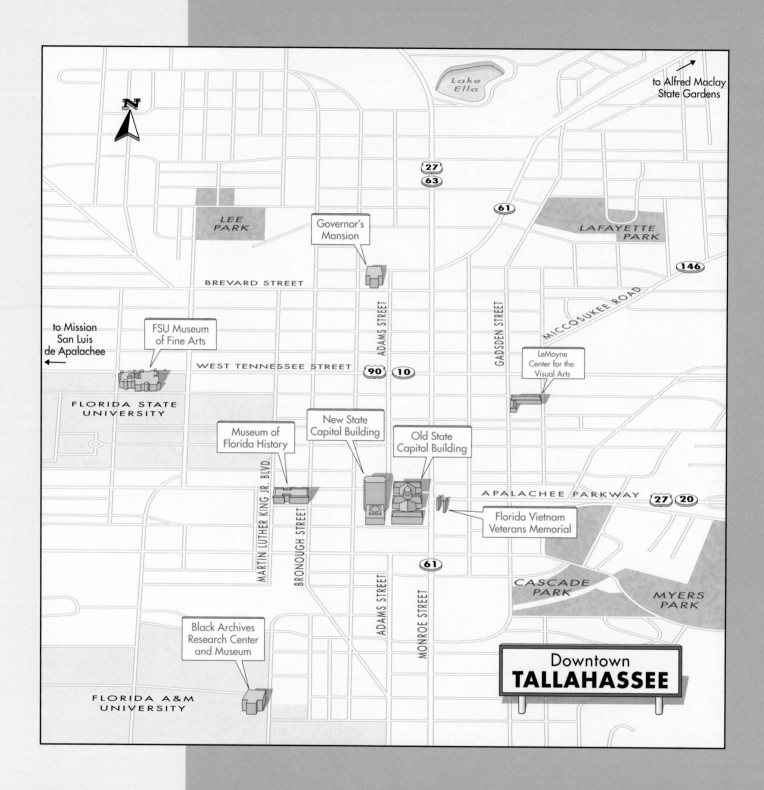

to Alfred Maclay
State Gardens

Lake
Ella

N

27
63

61

LEE
PARK

LAFAYETTE
PARK

146

Governor's
Mansion

BREVARD STREET

ADAMS STREET

GADSDEN STREET

MICCOSUKEE ROAD

to Mission
San Luis
de Apalachee

FSU Museum
of Fine Arts

WEST TENNESSEE STREET

90 10

LeMoyne
Center for the
Visual Arts

FLORIDA STATE
UNIVERSITY

Museum of
Florida History

New State
Capitol Building

Old State
Capitol Building

MARTIN LUTHER KING JR. BLVD.

BRONOUGH STREET

APALACHEE PARKWAY

27 20

Florida Vietnam
Veterans Memorial

61

CASCADE
PARK

MYERS
PARK

ADAMS STREET

MONROE STREET

Black Archives
Research Center
and Museum

FLORIDA A&M
UNIVERSITY

Downtown
TALLAHASSEE

100 types of camellias, plus brilliant azaleas, and exotic Florida plant life. You can also hike or bike on the nature trails there.

Two nearby attractions are also important to visit. The Florida Caverns State Park in Marianna is only twenty minutes from Tallahassee. These beautiful caverns delight visitors with dramatic displays of rock formations. You can also swim, row in a canoe, or ride a horse in the park. Wakulla Springs State Park is fifteen miles from Tallahassee. The park features one of the world's largest and deepest fresh water springs. Around the spring is 3,000 acres of forest. More than 150 kinds of birds live there, from purple gallinule to ospreys. Alligators and turtles sun themselves on rocks. Besides swimming and picnicking in the park, you can take guided river boat tours and view this unspoiled wilderness. You can also ride in a glass-bottom boat to see animals and plants that live underwater.

CHAPTER FIVE

THE PEOPLE AND PLACES OF FLORIDA

Snow White and the dwarves entertain visitors at Florida's most popular theme park, Walt Disney World.

(opposite)
This Miccosukee woman displays the traditional crafts she has made to sell to tourists. She sews colorful designs into a blanket.

Florida continues to grow at a rapid rate. A recent estimate puts Florida's population at more than 18 million people. About 85 of every 100 people live in a city. The major cities are Jacksonville, Miami, Tampa, Saint Petersburg, Hialeah, Orlando, and Fort Lauderdale. Of those cities, only Orlando is not on the coast.

Florida's population is mostly of European descent. Almost fifteen out of a hundred people is African-American. There are also large groups of Hispanics, Greek Americans, and Haitians. Cubans and Haitians most often live along the southeastern coast. The Cuban neighborhood in Miami is called "Little Havana," after Cuba's capital city.

The Native American population numbers about 36,000 and is mostly Seminole and Miccosukee. The Seminoles organized their own government and began officially calling themselves the Seminole Tribe of

Florida in 1957. Seminoles have two large reservations in South Florida: the Brighton Reservation near Lake Okeechobee and the Big Cypress Reservation to the northeast of Big Cypress National Preserve. In addition, they have other reservations, including Hollywood, Immokalee, and Fort Pierce. Some Seminoles refused to join the newly formed tribe and were officially recognized by the U.S. government in 1962 as the Miccosukee Tribe. The Miccosukee live on reserved lands in Alligator Alley and Krome Avenue.

Some Seminoles work on farms or help repair roads. Others run businesses that attract tourists, such as casinos, bingo games, hotels, and craft shops. Many also work as guides for people taking tours of the Everglades. Both Native American groups produce various fine crafts for sale, such as traditional dolls, clothing, and baskets. The Miccosukee also have gift shops, restaurants, and a casino.

The Hispanic Influence

Florida is a bilingual—two-language—state. Most store and street signs in Miami and Tampa are written in both Spanish and English. When people vote in Miami or Tampa, the voting ballots are printed in both English and Spanish.

Hispanic culture is found everywhere in Florida. Holy Week festivals in Saint Augustine, Latin-style Halloween in Tampa, and Carnaval in Miami are alive with bright colors and the rhythms of Latino bands. At night, Miami rocks to salsa music. In the day, older Cuban men often play dominoes in street cafes and drink strong Cuban coffee. Typical Cuban food found in Miami and elsewhere include *arroz con pollo* (roast chicken and rice), *picadillo* (beef stew), and *paella* (seafood and rice).

Cuban Calle Ocho dancers perform at Carnaval in Miami.

This recipe makes two tall glasses of smoothie.

FLORIDA CITRUS SMOOTHIE

1 tablespoon olive oil
1 medium banana
1/2 cup pineapple chunks
1 cup Florida orange juice
1 cup vanilla yogurt
1 cup ice

1. Put all ingredients in a blender and put on the blender's lid.
2. Whip together on purée speed until smooth, about 1-2 minutes.
3. Pour into a tall glass. Add a wedge of orange to your smoothie—and enjoy!

These elderly citizens enjoy playing shuffleboard in the Florida sunshine.

About two of every five Floridians are 65 years old or older. Florida is a popular place for elderly people to move because of the mild winters. Some seniors only "winter" in Florida. They come in November and leave in April. These part-time Floridians are called "snowbirds" because they take airplanes back to their homes in northern states when spring comes.

WORKING IN FLORIDA

Most workers in Florida work in stores or warehouses and in service businesses, such as hotels, motels, health care, or restaurants. Just over two of every ten workers work in stores, while five of every ten people provide services. One reason for the high number of service workers is the large tourist industry in Florida.

Tourism

Tourism is the business of providing food, housing, and entertainment for Florida's many visitors. So many tourists come to Florida that they spend about $65 billion each year. Can you guess which tourist spot

One of the joys of visiting Disney World is the possibility of a surprise appearance by Mickey and Minnie.

attracts the most visitors? It's Disney World, which covers 30,500 acres. However, Florida's beaches, historic sites, beautiful parks, and outdoor sports also keep tourists busy hiking, scuba diving, and surfing.

Farming and Fishing

Oranges and grapefruits make Florida farmers world-famous citrus growers. Throughout the state, more than 70 million citrus trees provide oranges, grapefruits, lemons, limes, tangelos, and kumquats. Florida produces three-fourths of all the oranges grown in the United States.

Florida has more than 42,000 farms. They supply much of the United States with fresh produce during the year. The second largest food crop after oranges is tomatoes. Other important crops include lettuce, strawberries, melons, bananas, soybeans for oil, peanuts, pecans, corn, cotton, oats, and celery.

Cattle ranches in the central highlands make the state a leading cattle producer. Florida farmers also raise hogs and broiler chickens. There is a small amount of dairy farming in Florida.

Commercial fishers catch bass, grouper, red snapper, bluefish, and mackerel. About three-fifths of all red snapper sold in the United States comes from Florida waters. Shellfish—shrimp, lobster, clams, oysters, and blue crabs—account for more than half the fishing industry catch in the state.

The lumber industry in the northern part of Florida is a small but active part of the state's economy. Softwoods, like pine, are cut for pulp and papermaking. Sap from Florida's pine forests is used to make turpentine and resin.

Fishers throw their nets out to find shrimp.

Manufacturing and Industry

The state's major industries include processing food, building transportation and electrical equipment, mining chemicals, manufacturing

EXTRA! EXTRA!

Florida produces more fresh tomatoes than any other state. California comes in second.

FIND OUT MORE

Many minerals are mined in Florida. How are Florida's mining products used?

This photo shows oranges being packaged in a factory. They will be sold in stores all around the world. Florida is the world's second-largest producer of oranges and orange juice. The country of Brazil is first.

paper products, and making cigars. Citrus products—frozen, canned, or packaged orange or grapefruit juice, jellies, and marmalades—are the major food products. Florida's factories also process and package coffee from South America, meat and dairy products from cattle and chicken ranches, and shrimp and other seafood.

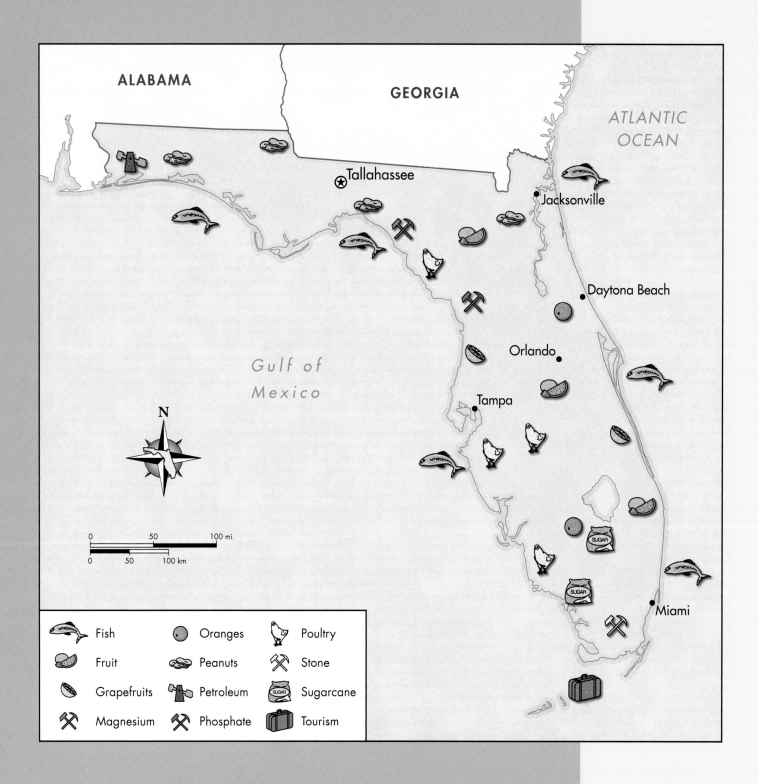

ALABAMA

GEORGIA

ATLANTIC OCEAN

Tallahassee

Jacksonville

Daytona Beach

Orlando

Gulf of Mexico

Tampa

Miami

N

| 0 | 50 | 100 mi. |
| 0 | 50 | 100 km |

Fish
Fruit
Grapefruits
Magnesium

Oranges
Peanuts
Petroleum
Phosphate

Poultry
Stone
Sugarcane
Tourism

SUGAR

Mining is important in Florida. Almost three-fourths of all phosphate produced in the United States is mined near Dunellon. Phosphate is used for making fertilizer. Florida is also the largest U.S. producer of zirconium, staurolite, and fuller's earth (used to make cat litter). Sand and gravel, limestone, dolomite, and clay are also valued mining products.

TAKE A TOUR OF FLORIDA

A tour of every attraction in Florida could take a year or more. There is plenty to do in this state. Miles of clean beaches provide swimming, sailing, parasailing, scuba diving, and fishing. People who would rather play golf than play in the Gulf have more than 130 golf courses on both sides of the peninsula to choose from. There are hundreds of museums, theme parks, amusement parks, and national and state parks.

Florida's professional sports fans support teams in football, basketball, baseball, soccer, and even hockey. Miami hosts the Dolphins football team and the Heat basketball team. Tampa Bay has football's Buccaneers and Jacksonville has its Jaguars. Orlando fans rave over the Magic basketball team. Major league baseball teams are the Florida Marlins in Miami, and the Tampa Bay Devil Rays in Saint Petersburg. Twenty professional teams hold spring training camps in Florida. Long before the season starts, Port St. Lucie fans are on their feet cheering homeruns by their favorite Mets batters.

Jai alai players throw a hard ball at about 150 miles (241 km) per hour.

Florida also has *jai alai*, dog racing, and horse racing. Jai alai is similar to handball, but players wear a long basket or *cesta* on one hand. Players catch the ball in the cesta and throw it back against the court's high walls. Greyhounds race on Florida's many dog tracks. Horseracing takes place at the famous Hialeah race track, near Miami.

Let's begin our state tour in Jacksonville, Florida's largest city. For history fans, the American Lighthouse Museum displays hundreds of lighthouses—in miniature, of course! The Kingsley Plantation reminds visitors of Florida's role as a slave-holding state. Jacksonville's Museum

The skyscrapers of Jacksonville reflect beautifully off the clear water.

of Science and History traces Florida's past from days of Spanish rule to the present.

Be sure to visit Jacksonville's zoo. More than 800 birds, reptiles, and mammals make their homes there. The Okavango Village, designed especially for children, features an authentic African village setting. Learn what it's like to live where lions prowl in your front yard!

Head south to Saint Augustine, the oldest permanent city in the United States. Visit the oldest wooden schoolhouse in the United States.

You'll discover just how big and roomy your classroom is. Duck your head—the doorway is not even six feet high! Nearby, Castillo de San Marcos looks out over Saint Augustine Inlet. Stand by cannons that are over three hundred years old, and imagine being the first to see the English coming to attack!

From a tower of Castillo de San Marcos, you can look for miles out into Matanzas Bay. This is the oldest masonry fort in the United States.

Crowds watch a killer whale performing at Sea World.

FIND OUT MORE

An important tourist site in Florida is the Kennedy Space Center. The Center has a museum with displays about exploring space, astronauts, and rockets. What might people learn at the Space Center?

Traveling southwest to Orlando, make a stop at Silver Springs first. You'll see the amazing underwater life in the springs—all through the floor of your glass-bottom boat! Go southwest to Orlando, where the most popular sites are Disney World, Epcot Center, Sea World, and Universal Studios. Enjoy the thrills of Disney World's Space Mountain or a more relaxing trip in an underwater submarine. Watch seals, dolphins, and orcas at Sea World. Then, learn how your favorite movies are made at Universal Studios! Not far from Orlando is Cypress Gardens, where you can see world famous water ski shows and enjoy beautiful gardens. Then make one more stop at Weeki Wachee Springs to check out live mermaids perform underwater.

Due east from Orlando are Cape Canaveral, the Kennedy Space Center, and NASA headquarters. If you've always dreamed of traveling through space, you'll enjoy visiting the Astronaut Hall of Fame and learning about people who've lived your dreams.

In southern Florida, dip your canoe paddles into the waters of Everglades National Park. Watch out—that "log" you hit could be an alligator! At the bottom of the state, put on your snorkel and fins. You'll want a close-up view of the underwater wonders of Biscayne National Park.

At the gateway to the Gulf of Mexico lies a string of islands called the Florida Keys, dozens of tiny islands ranging from Key Largo near Miami to Key West and the Dry Tortugas. This area is great for fishing, sailing, or just lying on the beach.

To cross from the east to the west, travelers take the Everglades Parkway, also known as Alligator Alley—for obvious reasons. From Naples northward, the beaches are on the Gulf of Mexico. Shell seeking,

The space shuttle *Atlantis* takes off from its launching pad.

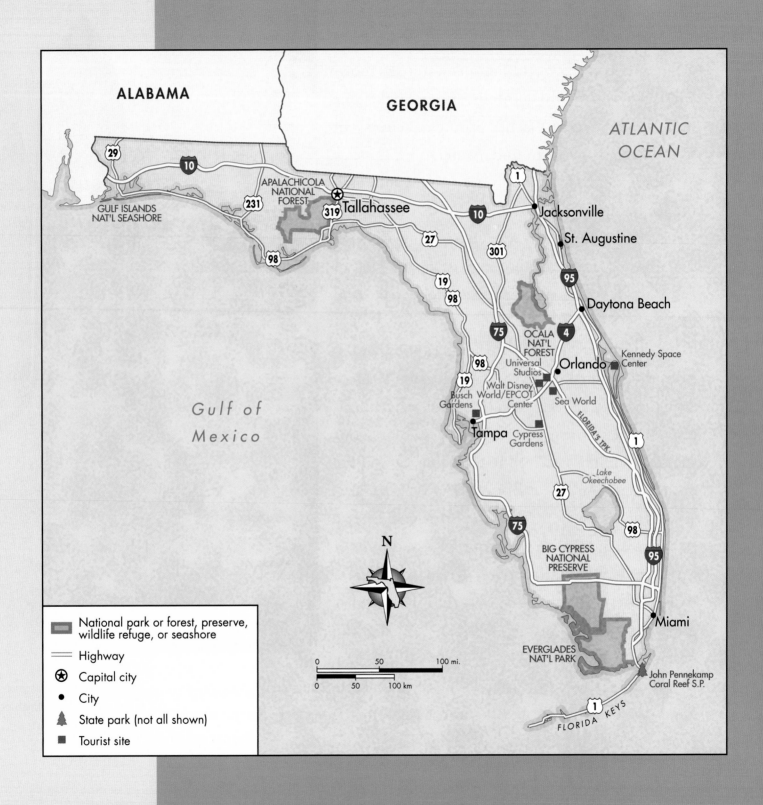

ALABAMA

GEORGIA

ATLANTIC OCEAN

(29)
(10)
GULF ISLANDS NAT'L SEASHORE
APALACHICOLA NATIONAL FOREST
(231)
(319) ⭐ Tallahassee
(98)
(1)
(10) ● Jacksonville
(27)
● St. Augustine
(301)
(95)
(19)
(98)
● Daytona Beach
(75)
OCALA NAT'L FOREST
(4)
Kennedy Space Center ■
(98)
Universal Studios ■
● Orlando
(19)
Busch Gardens ■
Walt Disney World/EPCOT Center ■
Sea World
■ Tampa
Cypress Gardens
FLORIDA'S TPK.
(1)
Lake Okeechobee
(27)
Gulf of Mexico
(75)
(98)
(95)
BIG CYPRESS NATIONAL PRESERVE

N

EVERGLADES NAT'L PARK
● Miami

John Pennekamp Coral Reef S.P. 🌲

(1) FLORIDA KEYS

0   50   100 mi.
0   50   100 km

National park or forest, preserve, wildlife refuge, or seashore
═══ Highway
⭐ Capital city
● City
🌲 State park (not all shown)
■ Tourist site

66

fishing, and water sports of all kinds are popular along the Gulf Coast. If you love shells, Sanibel Island is the place for you. You can pick shells up by the handful on Sanibel.

The Suncoast Sea Bird Sanctuary protects terns, pelicans, and other sea birds. There is also a manatee protection project that keeps these gentle sea cows safe from harm.

FIND OUT MORE

The Key deer is only found in the Florida Keys. This deer is small—only about two feet tall—and on the endangered species list. What do you think Florida should do to preserve this animal's habitat?

One of the pleasures of visiting the beach is feeding the seagulls.

A trip to Tampa should include visits to Busch Gardens and the Museum of Science and Industry. Busch Gardens gives you the best of both worlds: thrilling roller coaster and water rides, as well as a nature park where koalas, white tigers, and exotic birds live and play. The Museum of Science and Industry features more than two hundred hands-on exhibits. Among the best is the experience of surviving a Gulf Coast hurricane—scary, wet, and windy!

Circus fans must stop at the Ringling Brothers Circus in Sarasota. If you think you're funny—meet some of the future clowns at the clown school, also in Sarasota.

Along the Panhandle region, you'll find beaches, biking, and canoeing. Gentle currents encourage even beginning paddlers to canoe through the area's many waterways.

Florida has more attractions than most people have time to see. There are 110 state parks, 16.5 million acres of state forestland, and dozens of national monuments and historic treasures. A two-day visit to the Castillo de San Marcos in Saint Augustine and the John F. Kennedy Space Center spans Florida's history from Spanish settlement in 1565 to modern-day rocket launches to the moon.

(opposite)
No visit to Busch Gardens would be complete without a ride on a superfast roller coaster.

FLORIDA ALMANAC

Statehood date and number: March 3, 1845, 27th state

State seal: A Seminole woman scattering flowers in the water. Behind her are sabal palm trees, a river, and a steamboat. The background is blue with yellow rays of the sun. Adopted: 1868, revised 1985

State flag: A white background with a diagonal cross of red bars. The bars represent the Confederacy. The state seal is in the center. Adopted: 1899

Geographic center: Hernando, 12 miles (19 km) NNW of Brooksville

Total area/rank: 65,755 sq miles (170,304 sq km) 22nd

Coastline/rank: 1,350 miles (2,173 km)/second after Alaska

Borders: Alabama, Georgia, Gulf of Mexico, Atlantic Ocean

Latitude and longitude: 24°30' to 31°N and 80° to 87°28'W

Highest/lowest elevation: Walton County, 345 feet (105 m)/all coastal areas, sea level

Hottest/coldest temperature: 109°F (43°C), Monticello, June 29, 1931/-2°F (-19°C), Tallahassee, February 13, 1899

Average annual precipitation: 55 inches (140 cm)

Land area/rank: 53,927 sq miles (139,670 sq km) 26th

Inland water area: 4,672 sq miles (12,100 sq km)

Population/rank: 15,982,378 (2000 census)/4th

Origin of state name: Ponce de León called the land *Pascua Florida*, or "flowery Easter."

State capital: Tallahassee

Largest city: Jacksonville

Counties: 67

State government: 40 Senators, 120 Representatives

Major rivers/lakes: Okeechobee, Lake George, Lake Apopka, Cypress Lake, Spring Lake, Lake Kissimmee, Lake Griffin, Lake Harris, and Lake Ocklawaha
Over 1700 rivers, streams, and creeks. Saint Johns River, Ochlockonee, Apalachicola, Suwannee, Kissimmee, and the Everglades.

Farm products: Citrus fruits (oranges, grapefruits, lemons, limes, kumquats, tangerines, tangelos), tomatoes, lettuce, cucumbers, green beans, sugarcane, soybeans,

cantaloupe and other melons, strawberries, tobacco, cotton, pecans, peanuts, cabbage, and corn

Livestock: beef cattle, poultry and poultry products, pork, and race horses

Manufactured products: Paper, printing, electrical equipment, scientific instruments, chemicals, machinery, processed foods, and avionics

Mining: Phosphate, limestone, dolomite, sand, gravel, titanium, magnesium, gypsum

Commercial fishing: Shrimp, crab, swordfish, bass, catfish, crappie, red snapper, bluefish, dolphin, and sponges, among others

Animal: Florida panther

Beverage: Orange juice

Bird: Mockingbird

Butterfly: Zebra longwing

Flower: Orange blossom

Freshwater fish: Largemouth bass

Gem: Moonstone

Insect: Praying mantis

Marine mammal: Manatee

Motto: In God We Trust

Nickname: The Sunshine State

Saltwater fish: Atlantic sailfish

Saltwater mammal: Porpoise

Shell: Horse conch

Song: "The Swanee River," words and music by Stephen Foster (1851)

State Fair: Tampa, each February

Stone: Agatized coral

Tree: Sabal palm

TIMELINE

FLORIDA STATE HISTORY

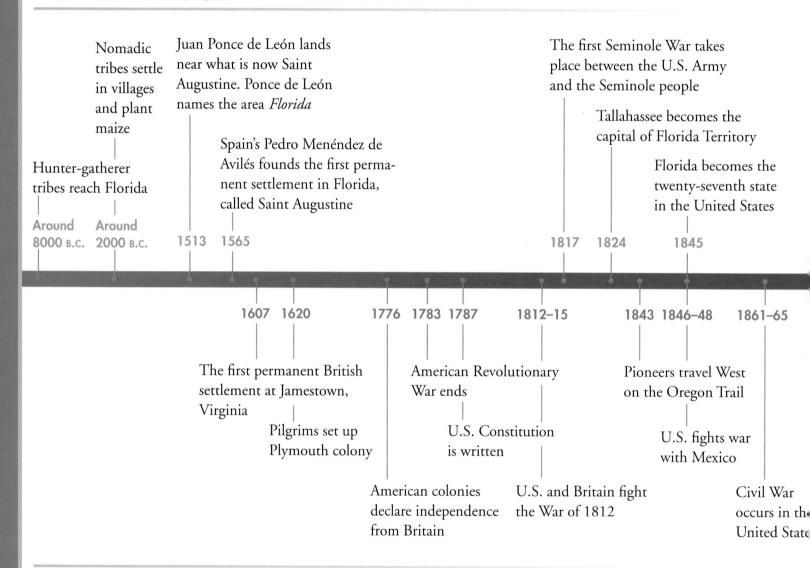

Nomadic tribes settle in villages and plant maize

Juan Ponce de León lands near what is now Saint Augustine. Ponce de León names the area *Florida*

The first Seminole War takes place between the U.S. Army and the Seminole people

Tallahassee becomes the capital of Florida Territory

Spain's Pedro Menéndez de Avilés founds the first perma-nent settlement in Florida, called Saint Augustine

Florida becomes the twenty-seventh state in the United States

Hunter-gatherer tribes reach Florida

Around 8000 B.C.   Around 2000 B.C.   1513   1565   1817   1824   1845

1607   1620   1776   1783   1787   1812–15   1843   1846–48   1861–65

The first permanent British settlement at Jamestown, Virginia

American Revolutionary War ends

Pioneers travel West on the Oregon Trail

Pilgrims set up Plymouth colony

U.S. Constitution is written

U.S. fights war with Mexico

American colonies declare independence from Britain

U.S. and Britain fight the War of 1812

Civil War occurs in the United State

UNITED STATES HISTORY

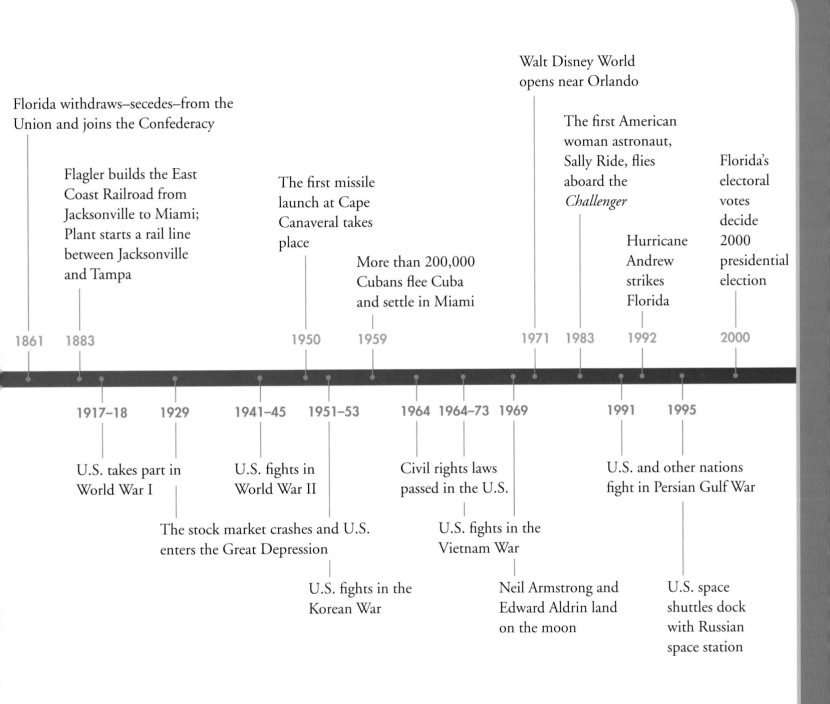

Walt Disney World
opens near Orlando

Florida withdraws—secedes—from the
Union and joins the Confederacy

The first American
woman astronaut,
Sally Ride, flies
aboard the
Challenger

Florida's
electoral
votes
decide
2000
presidential
election

Flagler builds the East
Coast Railroad from
Jacksonville to Miami;
Plant starts a rail line
between Jacksonville
and Tampa

The first missile
launch at Cape
Canaveral takes
place

More than 200,000
Cubans flee Cuba
and settle in Miami

Hurricane
Andrew
strikes
Florida

1861   1883   1950   1959   1971   1983   1992   2000

1917–18   1929   1941–45   1951–53   1964   1964–73   1969   1991   1995

U.S. takes part in
World War I

U.S. fights in
World War II

Civil rights laws
passed in the U.S.

U.S. and other nations
fight in Persian Gulf War

The stock market crashes and U.S.
enters the Great Depression

U.S. fights in the
Vietnam War

U.S. fights in the
Korean War

Neil Armstrong and
Edward Aldrin land
on the moon

U.S. space
shuttles dock
with Russian
space station

73

GALLERY OF FAMOUS FLORIDIANS

Mary McLeod Bethune

(1875–1955)

Educator and founder of Bethune-Cookman College. Served as director of the Division of Negro Affairs of the National Youth Administration under President Franklin D. Roosevelt.

Fernando Bujones

(1955–)

Cuban-American ballet dancer. A former principal dancer with the American Ballet Theatre. Born in Miami.

Jacqueline Cochran

(1912–1980)

Businesswoman and pilot. Helped organize the Women's Air Force Service Pilots during World War II.

Gloria Estefan

(1957–)

Singer and leader of the musical group Miami Sound Machine. Born in Havana, Cuba, but lived most of her life in Miami.

Zora Neale Hurston

(1901–1960)

Writer known for portraying African-American life. Her books include *Mules and Men* (1935) and *Their Eyes Were Watching God* (1937). Born in Eatonville.

Andrew Jackson

(1767–1845)

Governor of Florida Territory and United States president.

James Weldon Johnson

(1871–1938)

Writer, poet, teacher, and civil rights leader. He was the first African-American executive secretary of the NAACP. Born in Jacksonville.

Ruth Bryan Owen

(1885–1954)

First woman from a Southern state elected to the House of Representatives (1929), and a U.S. diplomat (1933).

Marjorie Kinnan Rawlings

(1896-1953)

Author of books about rural life. Wrote *The Yearling* (1939), which received the Pulitzer Prize. Lived in Cross Creek, near Gainesville.

Janet Reno

(1938–)

First female U.S. Attorney General. Born in Miami.

John Ringling

(1866–1936)

One of five brothers who owned the Ringling Brothers Circus. Established the circus in Sarasota.

GLOSSARY

amendment: a change or addition in a law or document

cabinet: a group of advisors to a governor or president

capital: a city that is the center of state or national government

capitol: the building in which a government meets

climate: an area's average weather conditions

constitution: a document that sets out the basic rules and laws that run a government

defendant: a person accused of committing a crime

ecology: the balance of plant and animal life in a region

economy: how people make money

felony: a serious crime, such as murder or theft

governor: an elected person who heads the executive branch of state government

hurricane: a storm that forms over an ocean or sea

manufacturing: making products, such as cars or lamps

peninsula: a body of land surrounded on three sides by water

plantation: a large farm on which one main crop is grown

population: the number and mix of people in a region

reservation: public land set aside by the government for use by Native Americans

secede: to withdraw from a group

sinkhole: a hole formed when underground running water eats away the rock through which the water passes

slavery: system in which people are treated as property and work without pay or freedom

tourism: the business of providing hotels, restaurants, and entertainment for visitors

transportation: a system of roads, trains, busses, and airports

unemployment: the number of people looking for work who can't find jobs

FOR MORE INFORMATION

Web Sites

Florida Museum of Natural History
http://www.flmnh.ufl.edu/
A tour of fossil photo galleries and online exhibits about Florida's animal and plant life.

Florida State Symbols and Emblem
http://www.netstate.com/states/symb/fl_symb.htm
Provides a chart of basic statistics and other information.

Online Sunshine—Florida's Legislature
http://www.leg.state.fl.us/
A visit to the Florida state legislature.

Books

Lourie, Peter. *Everglades: Buffalo Tiger and the River of Grass.* Honesdale, PA: Boyds Mills Press, 1994.

Morgan, Cheryl K. *The Everglades.* Mahwah, NJ: Troll, 1990.

Wills, Charles A. *A Historical Album of Florida.* Brookfield, CT: Millbrook Press, 1994.

Addresses

Florida Division of Tourism
126 Van Buren Street
Tallahassee, FL 32399-2000

Governor's Office
Plaza Level, The Capitol
Tallahassee, FL 32399-0001

Miami/Metro-Dade Department of Planning
Research Division
111 NW First Street, Suite 1220
Miami, FL 33128

INDEX